See Through Education: Shakespeare

The 'See Through' approach to

The 'See Through Shakespeare' project:
number of very different schools. We s
themes, language, context and genre i
challenging, culminating in a performa..... ....
class.

We began with story-telling and discussion of the choices made by Shakespeare about what to show and what to tell. Students identified aspects which, in their view, posed problems or were alienating. Out of such discussion came agreement about a way in which these issues could be tackled in performance – using narrators to present the action, comment on the characters and find a line through ambiguities and complexities. The characters of the narrators themselves were chosen to reflect or provide a context for some aspect of their play.

This approach provides both a practical route into the study of the Shakespeare plays chosen as set texts and an opportunity to gain an appreciation of other Shakespeare plays to use for comparison and to deepen understanding. Students are helped to focus on Shakespeare's choices – key words and images, for example, and the use of iambic pentameter to suggest pace and significant pauses. The text can either be used simply within an English class with the students reading aloud, developed into a performance within Drama or run as a cross-curricular project.

Having the goal of performance has always concentrated minds wonderfully, as well as giving opportunities for students to develop and display skills across a broad spectrum of activities, including art and design, music and information technology, as well as acting and directing. The scope for independent learning, teamwork, leadership and communication is extensive. A workshop approach means that the final performance does not rely on specialised and expensive resources.

Patricia Metham

Patricia currently works with Primary and Secondary schools across South East England to improve standards and student attainment. Previously, she was an HMI and the National Lead for English and Literacy at Ofsted.

As a headteacher, Patricia led a range of UK and International schools including Roedean, East Sussex and The Regent's School, Thailand.

Her original degree was in Drama, English and History. She has published a series of play commentaries and notes (as Patricia Hern) as part of the Methuen Student Editions, including: Harold Pinter's *Birthday Party*', Tennessee Williams's *Streetcar Named Desire*, and Edward Bond's *Lear*.

Doing Hamlet: Teachers' Notes

How to use this text

This adaptation can be read aloud by a class with no rehearsal or preparation. A cast list is provided so all the parts can be easily allocated. It is important to read the stage directions aloud as they are additions for this series; Shakespeare's folio texts have very few explicit stage directions or commentary. The stage directions and the modern scenes interlacing Shakespeare's original text help illuminate the characters' motivations, the historical and literary context of the play, and the dominant themes.

If you have more time, or are working within a drama setting, the whole play, or a selection of scenes, can be prepared by the students for an in-class presentation or a larger performance.

Ideas for preparation activities and homeworks are provided so you can extend the use of this adaptation, as you want, to strengthen students' understanding.

****

Meeting National Curriculum expectations

These links focus on the English National Curriculum but can be adapted to match other curricular.

Key Stage 2

The overarching aim for English in the national curriculum is to promote high standards of language and literacy by equipping pupils with a strong command of the spoken and written language, and to develop their love of literature through widespread reading for enjoyment. The national curriculum for Key Stage 2 English aims to ensure that all pupils:

- read easily, fluently and with good understanding

- develop the habit of reading widely and often, for both pleasure and information

- acquire a wide vocabulary, an understanding of grammar and knowledge of linguistic conventions for reading, writing and spoken language

- appreciate our rich and varied literary heritage

- write clearly, accurately and coherently, adapting their language and style in and for a range of contexts, purposes and audiences

- use discussion in order to learn; they should be able to elaborate and explain clearly their understanding and ideas

- are competent in the arts of speaking and listening, making formal presentations, demonstrating to others and participating in debate.

This approach to *Hamlet* is designed to extend pupils' awareness of our literary heritage, to use discussion to share and develop ideas and to develop confidence and competence in the arts of speaking and listening, role play and making formal presentations.

Key Stage 3 & 4

This approach provides both a practical route into the study of the Shakespeare play chosen as a set text – a requirement in Key Stage 3 and Key Stage 4 - and an opportunity to gain an appreciation of a second Shakespeare play to use for comparison with the chosen set text and to deepen understanding. Pupils are helped to focus on Shakespeare's choices – key words and images, for example, and the use of iambic pentameter to suggest pace and significant pauses.

National Curriculum:

'Pupils should be taught to understand and use the conventions for discussion and debate, as well as continuing to develop their skills in working collaboratively with their peers to discuss reading, writing and speech across the curriculum.'

'Pupils should be taught to speak confidently and effectively, including through improvising, rehearsing and performing play scripts and poetry in order to generate language and discuss language use and meaning, using role, intonation, tone, volume, mood, silence, stillness and action to add impact.'

GCSE English Literature subject content and assessment objectives, including the requirements for reading comprehension and reading critically:

- *literal and inferential comprehension*: understanding a word, phrase or sentence in context; exploring aspects of plot, characterization, events and settings;

distinguishing between what is stated explicitly and what is implied; explaining motivation, sequence of events, and the relationship between actions or events

- *critical reading*: identifying the theme and distinguishing between themes; supporting a point of view by referring to evidence in the text; recognising the possibility of and evaluating different responses to a text; using understanding of writers' social, historical and cultural contexts to inform evaluation; making an informed personal response that derives from analysis and evaluation of the text

- *evaluation of a writer's choice of vocabulary, grammatical and structural features*: analysing and evaluating how language (including figurative language), structure, form and presentation contribute to quality and impact; using linguistic and literary terminology for such evaluation (such as, but not restricted to, phrase, metaphor, metre, irony and persona, synecdoche, pathetic fallacy)

- *comparing texts*: comparing and contrasting texts studied, referring where relevant to theme, characterization, context (where known), style and literary quality; comparing two texts critically with respect to the above.

****

Using "Doing Hamlet"

A drama option: preparing for performance

This script can be developed into a performance whether through English, Drama, or as a cross-curricular project. As pupils work towards a performance, there needs to be time for discussion and, if they feel the need, adaptation of the script. If possible, pupils compose and perform music, as well as create a practical set and costumes, lighting plan and pre-performance PR. Ideally, a group takes responsibility for putting together a record of the progress from first rehearsals to final performance – video, blog, written logs. . .

In working towards performance, scripts can be used as much as needed rather than all lines having to be learnt.

If it is not practicable to make a public performance the end point of this project, an 'in-class' workshop approach to the text can work well. The scenes can be split between three mixed-ability groups: Prologue and scenes 1-4; scenes 5-9; and scene 10 to the end.

Each group should have a pupil as director; this is a role for those able to develop a coherent approach and to negotiate successfully with group members. He or she may also play a character. It remains important to have the discipline of an end point, when each group presents to the others, in sequence.

Dramatic use of iambic pentameters

The basic pentameter line has ten syllables; it can have eleven if the final syllable is not stressed (e.g. 'O villain, villain, smiling damned villain'). It may be helpful to think of each iambic pentameter line as music, written in five bars and with two beats to each bar. This sets an underlying rhythm that the dramatist can then use to dictate the pace of an exchange between characters – a line split between speakers indicates that the exchange is quick, with each speaker almost cutting across the previous speech. The dramatist can also leave a line with fewer than 10 syllables, to be followed by a complete line. This indicates a pause, when something has to be happening on stage. Such pauses are important and it is easy to miss them if simply reading a text aloud, not performing it.

An example of a pentameter split between characters, that indicates speed of response, comes when Laertes bursts into the court at Elsinore, full of fury.

Laertes: Where is my father?

Claudius: Dead.

Gertrude: But not by him (*indicating Claudius*).

An example of a pause created by the cutting short of one line that is then followed by a complete pentameter comes when Hamlet is leaving his mother, having killed Polonius.

Hamlet:

Good night. But go not to my uncle's bed.	(*A complete pentameter*)
For this same lord	(*4 spoken syllables – 6 'silent' beats*)
I do repent; but heaven hath pleased it so,	(*A complete pentameter*)
To punish me with this, and this with me.	

In performance, how is the pause created by the six 'missing' syllables to be used? What is happening? The pause can come either before or after Hamlet's words 'For this same lord'. It *must* come before 'I do repent'.

Possibly the most critical pause is written into Act 5, scene 2. Claudius has dropped poison into a goblet of wine that he intends for Hamlet. To his consternation, Gertrude picks it up to drink from. He tries to stop her. There are five beats without dialogue: what is happening?

Gertrude: (*Taking the poisoned cup.*) The Queen carouses to thy fortune, Hamlet.

Claudius: Gertrude, do not drink. (*This line has 5 spoken syllables and 5 'silent' beats.*)

During the five beats of silence Shakespeare has written into the 10-beat iambic line, it must be made clear whether or not Gertrude suddenly recognizes that Claudius is as evil as Hamlet has claimed and that there is something very wrong with the wine she is holding. If she understands that, then her decision to drink the wine is heroic; she sacrifices herself to save her son. In that case, it may be Hamlet she asks to pardon her – for not believing him when he spoke of his father being murdered and for continuing to stay beside Claudius despite Hamlet's opposition. However, she could simply be determined to have the wine because she likes wine and is annoyed by her husband telling her what not to do, so her reply is to him, and not Hamlet, in a petulantly challenging kind of way.

Gertrude: I will, my lord, I pray you pardon me.   (*This is a full iambic line.*)

A brief outline of how the project can be managed

- Begin by watching a film or theatre performance of the whole play, or listening to a well-written version of the story.

- Ask pupils, working in small groups or pairs, to come up with one or two questions they would like to have asked Shakespeare himself about any aspect of the play. Post these on a 'working wall' as points of reference. Invite possible answers. Add those to the 'working wall' if, after discussion, they are thought to be worth keeping in mind.

- Set groups to explore agreed topics and report back to the class – what Elizabethan theatres looked like; how players were organised by 1600 (when it seems likely *Hamlet* was first performed); a brief outline of Shakespeare's life, perhaps presented as an interview with him; any other lines of enquiry arising from discussion.

- Read through *Doing Hamlet*. If there are questions on the 'working wall' that have not been covered, agree where they can be integrated and what answers should be suggested by the Players as narrators as well as participants. You may find it helpful to put a glossary of particularly challenging words on the board at the start of each section as a support for less able or less confident pupils.

- As a way into the drama, ask each group to choose two especially significant or dramatic moments from their section and create a freeze-frame or tableau for each. One of the group should act as narrator, explaining what the freeze-frame is presenting. These should then be presented by the groups, following the sequence of events in the play.

Homework

- Each pupil may write an answer to one of the questions on the 'working wall', as Shakespeare.

- Each pupil may keep a working log-book or portfolio, regularly updated. It would include a range of writing activities: diary entries (either the pupil's own experience, or written in the person of a character in the play); letters from one character to another; self-evaluation by the pupils of their personal learning and progress; background research…

- Pupils can explore the meaning and use of key words from the text, such as: 'knavish'/'knavery'; 'noble'; 'honour'; 'mad'/'distracted'/'madness'; 'true'/'false'.

- Find two examples of a single iambic pentameter line split between characters, and explain the effect. Also find examples where a single iambic pentameter line is left incomplete, with the following line having the full ten or eleven syllables. Explain the significance of this in performance.

- More-able pupils could explore how Machiavelli's observations about the values and action of a successful ruler (see below) might be applied to Claudius, and even to Hamlet.

****

Resources

Possible sources for Shakespeare's 'Hamlet'

- Amleth is the central figure in a medieval Scandinavian legend. He is the son of Koll, Ruler of Jutland, who killed the King of Norway and married his daughter, Gerutha. Koll was later murdered by his brother, Feng, who then married Gerutha. Fearing for his life, Amleth pretended to be mad but Feng was unconvinced and tried to catch him out. Amongst Feng's schemes was to lure Amleth into a relationship with his foster-sister, but this failed. When Amleth stabbed a spy sent by Feng to eavesdrop on a conversation between Amleth and his mother, Feng sent him to Britain along with two attendants, who had a message to the King of Britain instructing him to kill Amleth. Amleth changed the message to ensure that the attendants were killed and that he was married to the British King's daughter. Amleth and his bride returned to Jutland just as his supposed death was being celebrated at court. He drugged and killed the courtiers and stabbed Feng. Amleth was then declared King of Jutland. Ultimately, he was killed in a battle with the King of Denmark.

- This story is included in a French collection of tragic tales, published in 1572.

- Performance of an English stage version, now known as *Ur-Hamlet* (*Predecessor-Hamlet*), is referred to by a contemporary writer, Thomas Nashe, but the play-text has not survived.

- Philip Henslowe, a very successful theatre manager and businessman and a contemporary of Shakespeare, refers in his diary of 1594 to a performance of *Hamlet* by the Chamberlain's Men, Shakespeare's company. He does not describe this as a new play and it seems likely that the performance was of the earlier *Ur-Hamlet*.

Tragedy

It is important to remember that Shakespeare had a classical education. He knew his Aristotle! 'Pity and fear' – that's what we're meant to feel for a tragic hero. 'Pity' because we see he's got what it takes to be a good man, but he's also got a fatal weakness that eventually destroys him. And 'fear' because we know he's caught up in a deadly chain of events he can't escape.

Hamlet is an interesting tragic hero because he has a great deal in common with one of the best-known heroes of Greek classical tragedy – Orestes. This Greek model focuses on the deadly chain of events the hero can't escape. Essentially, there is nothing accidental about his suffering; his situation is unique to him and his dilemma is created by conflicting laws or moral imperatives between which he is trapped. Agamemnon, father of Orestes, is killed by Clytemnestra, mother of Orestes, partly to avenge his sacrificing of their daughter to the gods in order to get a wind to take his ships to Troy. As Agamemnon's son, Orestes *must* avenge his death – that is what the Laws of the Universe dictate. If he does not avenge his father's murder, he will create a disturbance in the universe, upset the balance of the Universe (known as diké) and he will be punished. On the other hand, to avenge his father's murder, he must kill his mother – and matricide is an unnatural act that will also upset dike. He cannot choose to do nothing – because 'doing nothing' means choosing not to avenge his father's assassination. After an agony of indecision, he kills his mother – and is then pursued by the Furies.

Hamlet feels that he is honour-bound to avenge his father's murder. He has not himself committed a crime – unlike Macbeth – but he will be destroyed by a sense of guilt and betrayal if he does not follow his destiny as the instrument of revenge/justice. Yet, to avenge his father, he must commit a dreadful crime – he must kill a king! And, for killing a king, he will then be killed. In 1600, the moral questions and, as importantly, political questions, posed by the killing of a king or queen were of immeasurable importance. Would it ever be justified? Even *thinking* about killing Elizabeth I was unforgivable! Yet she had signed the death warrant for Mary, Queen of Scots, and her grandfather, Henry VII, had killed Richard III, to gain the throne.

Revenge tragedy was a very popular theatrical form during the later C16th and early C17th. It worked within clear conventions which performers and audience understood.

From very early on in the piece, the audience is presented with a murder, at least one murderer and the person whose moral obligation it is to exact revenge for the murder because the victim was their parent or someone to whom they owed loyalty. The pattern was set by Thomas Kyd's play *The Spanish Tragedy*, written about ten years before Shakespeare's *Hamlet*. Amongst the devices in Kyd's play that Shakespeare incorporated into *Hamlet* are a ghost demanding vengeance and a play-within-a-play. Since the crime and the criminal are established at the start of the play, the challenge for the playwright is how to keep the action lively and the audience interested until finally the hero achieves his anticipated revenge – and as often as not dies in the process. Pretend or 'real' madness, accidental killings, mistaken identities and doomed loves were common devices.

Machiavelli 1469-1527 – The Prince

Nicolo Machiavelli was born, educated and became a senior diplomat in Renaissance Florence. For much of his life, he was on the winning side in the struggles between ambitious families for control of this wealthy and powerful city state, but in 1512 he was arrested on suspicion of conspiracy and tortured. He was released but did not return to political life. In his short, influential work, *The Prince*, completed in 1503 but not published until 1513, he drew on his experience in the service of the Medici family, dominant in Florence. His observations about the qualities, priorities and actions of a successful prince or ruler spread quickly across Europe at a time when power politics were evolving to meet new and urgent challenges of nationalistic and religious conflict. Machiavelli's ideas had reached England by the mid-1530s, when Henry VIII's decision to break away from the jurisdiction of the Pope in Rome and declare himself Head of the Church of England prompted intense review of where the power of a national leader was based and how it could be made secure. By the time Shakespeare was writing plays that deal with the rise and fall of kings and queens, 'Machiavellian' had come to mean an approach to politics and governance in which the end justified the means in the pursuit and exploitation of power. Shakespeare gives the phrase 'murderous Machiavell' in *Henry VI, Part 3* to Gloucester (later Richard III).

Machiavelli dedicated *The Prince* to 'the Magnificent Lorenzo Di Piero De' Medici'. The following quotations give a sense of Machiavelli's thinking about the characteristics of a successful ruler. He commented that anyone seizing power, possibly through assassination, should 'examine closely into all those injuries which it is necessary for him to inflict, and to do them all at one stroke so as not to have to repeat them daily' (Chapter 8). He argued that 'it is necessary for a prince wishing to hold his own to know how to do wrong, and to make use of it or not according to necessity' (Chapter 15). He developed this idea further: 'Upon this a question arises: whether it be better to be loved than feared or feared than loved? It may be answered that one should wish to be both, but, because it is difficult to unite them in one person, it is much safer to be feared than loved, when, of the two, either must be dispensed with. Because this is to be asserted in general of men, that they are ungrateful, fickle, false, cowardly, covetous, and as long as you succeed they are yours entirely; they will offer you their blood, property, life, and children, as is said above, when the need is far distant; but when it approaches they turn against you.' (Chapter 17) In ways that both Hamlet and his uncle, Claudius, understood well, the successful ruler must be able to deceive others. 'Everyone sees what you appear to be, few really know what you are, and those few dare not oppose themselves to the opinion of the many, who have the majesty of the state to defend them; and in the actions of all men, and especially of princes, which it is not prudent to challenge, one judges by the result.' (Chapter 18)

[These extracts are taken from The Project Gutenberg eBook of The Prince, by Nicolo Machiavelli. This eBook is for the use of anyone anywhere at no cost and with almost no restrictions. You may copy it, give it away or re-use it under the terms of the Project Gutenberg License included with this eBook or online at www.gutenberg.org Translator: W. K. Marriott. Produced by John Bickers & David Widger]

Playhouses – theatres – in Shakespeare's time

Before the reign of Elizabeth I, most public drama happened in towns and villages around the country and not in purpose-built playhouses or theatres. Mystery plays were performed by men who were not professional actors but craftsmen and traders who presented well-known stories from the Bible, usually during a religious festival such as Easter and Christmas. Morality plays, like *Everyman*, were used to present a moral lesson to be learnt and followed. These used stock characters, generally identified by their names, such as Worldly Goods and Good Deeds.

There were also bands of travelling performers, who would set up a temporary stage in the market place or in the courtyard of a coaching inn and act out mostly rather crude comedies, with dancing and juggling often included. They were seen as being outside respectable society – 'vagabonds, jugglers and tinkers'.

An important change came in the 1570s, when the Earl of Sussex – the Lord Chamberlain - became the patron and sponsor of a group of full-time actors, who toured the provinces and also performed at the court of Queen Elizabeth. Shakespeare later became a member of the Lord Chamberlain's Men. The Earl of Sussex set a trend; soon the Earl of Leicester became patron of another company of full-time performers. The patronage of such powerful men changed the status of actors and paved the way for more serious playwriting and performance, and led to investment in purpose-built playhouses in London. The distinction became critical when, in 1572, a royal decree tightened up the Poor Laws and made it clear that any travelling players not genuinely part of the household of a nobleman, and wearing his livery, would be arrested as vagabonds. Punishments ranged from whipping on a first offence to death on a third offence.

Playhouses during Shakespeare's life as an actor and playwright were either outdoor or indoor. The basic design of outdoor playhouses grew out of the coaching inn courtyards where performances had taken place in earlier times.

Indoor playhouses were of four kinds:

- those set up in the halls of university colleges or the Middle Temple in London

- those set up, without scenery, in the halls of great houses, like the hall of Hampton Court Palace;

- 'private' playhouses such as the Blackfriars;

- and playhouses with scenery, set up in formal or official halls, such as the Great Hall of Whitehall Palace.

The large, outdoor playhouses could accommodate up to 3,000, with many in the audience standing in front of and around the stage. To see what these playhouses were like, visit The Globe Theatre on Bankside in London, or its website. This theatre was built as far as possible to be a copy of The Globe Theatre in which Shakespeare and his company would have performed. The complex also includes a reconstruction of the kind of indoor theatre Shakespeare would have known. (This reconstruction is called the Sam Wannamaker Theatre.)

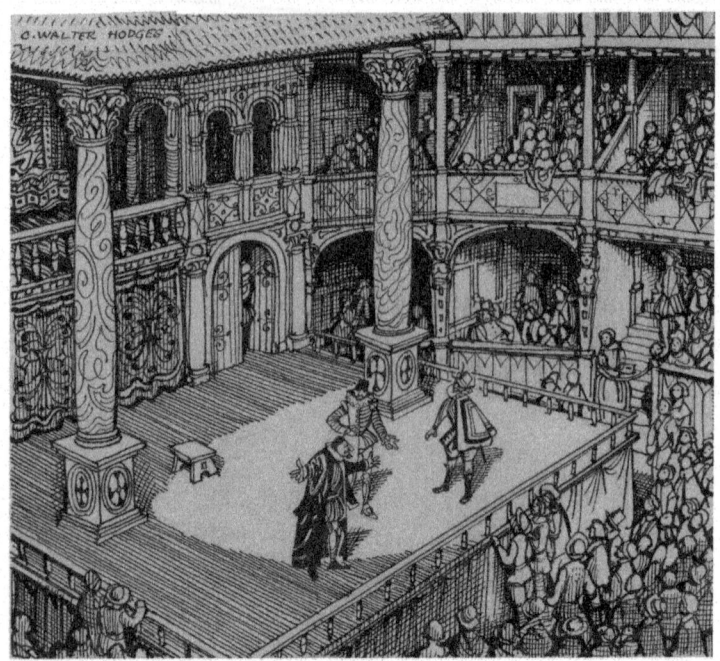

C. Walter Hodges' imagined reconstruction of Shakespeare's *Merchant of Venice*, act 1, scene 3, being performed in an Elizabethan theatre. Drawn for The Globe Restored, published by Ernest Benn, 1953. Folger Shakespeare Library ART Box H688 no.3.1

Shakespearean Time-frame

Date	Politics	Other events	Shakespeare
1558	Elizabeth I becomes Queen, succeeding her Catholic sister, Mary I.	The Church of England is re-established.	
1560		Puritanism takes root in England.	
1564		Christopher Marlowe is born. Galileo is born.	W.S. born (?)
1569		Mercator's world map for navigation is published.	
1570	Elizabeth I is excommunicated		
1572	Amendments to the Poor Laws require all travelling players to have noble patronage, to avoid their being punished as vagrants.	James Burbage and other actors write to the Earl of Leicester asking for his patronage and protection.	
1574		Elizabeth I grants a royal patent to Leicester's troupe of players.	
1576		James Burbage builds The Theatre.	
1577		Francis Drake sets off round the world.	
1582			W.S. marries Anne Hathaway.
1583		Queen's Company (Players) is formed.	Daughter Susanna is born.
1585		Actor Edward Alleyn leads the Chamberlain's Men	Twins Hamnet and Judith are born.
1587	Mary Queen of Scots is executed.	Thomas Kyd's *Spanish Tragedy* Marlowe's *Tamburlaine I*	W.S. signs legal papers in Stratford.

Date	Politics	Other events	Shakespeare
1588	The Spanish Armada is defeated. The Earl of Leicester dies.	Marlowe's *Tamburlaine II* and *Doctor Faustus* Sidney's *Arcadia* (poem)	W.S. is possibly touring as an actor.
1589		**Thomas Nashe refers to an English stage version of *Hamlet*, known as *Ur-Hamlet*, possibly by Kyd.**	
1590		Spenser's *Fairie Queene* (poem)	*Henry VI, Parts I, II & III* (completed 1592)
1591	Duke of Essex leads an expedition to Normandy.		*Henry VI Part I*
1592		Plague in London. Marlowe's *Edward II*	*The Comedy of Errors* *Richard III* *Sonnets*
1593		Marlowe is killed in a pub brawl.	*Titus Andronicus* *The Taming of the Shrew* *Venus and Adonis* (a narrative poem)
1594		Thomas Kyd dies. **Theatre-manager Philip Henslowe refers to a performance of *Hamlet* by the Chamberlain's Men (likely to be Kyd's *Ur-Hamlet*).**	W.S. joins The Lord Chamberlain's Men, with actor Richard Burbage and clown Will Kemp. *Two Gentlemen of Verona* *Love's Labour's Lost* *Romeo and Juliet* *Sonnets* *Rape of Lucrece* (a narrative poem)
1595			*Richard II* *A Midsummer Night's Dream* *Sonnets*
1596	Capture of Cadiz	Blackfriars Theatre opens (indoor theatre).	Shakespeare's father is granted a Coat of Arms. Hamnet dies. *The Merchant of Venice* *King John*

Date	Politics	Other events	Shakespeare
1597		Islands voyage by Earl of Southampton. Philip Henslowe builds the Rose Theatre.	W.S. buys New Place. *Henry IV, Parts I & II*
1598	Irish rebellion	Jonson's *Every Man in His Humour*	*Much Ado About Nothing*
1599	Essex is sent to Ireland as Lord Lieutenant and arrested on his return to England.	The Globe opens, owned by the Lord Chamberlain's Men and James Burbage.	*As You Like It* *Henry V* *Julius Caesar*
1600-01	Essex leads a revolt and is executed.	Henslowe builds The Fortune Theatre, for the Admiral's Men (rivals of the Lord Chamberlain's Men).	*Twelfth Night* **Hamlet** *The Merry Wives of Windsor*
1602			W.S. buys land in Stratford. *Troilus and Cressida*
1603	Elizabeth I dies. James VI of Scotland (son of Mary Queen of Scots) becomes James I of England.	The Chamberlain's Men become The King's Men, with the granting of a royal patent. Plague outbreak	*All's Well That Ends Well* W.S. and others in his company become Grooms of the Chamber, part of the royal household.
1604	Peace treaty with Spain		*Measure for Measure* *Othello*
1605	Gunpowder Plot		*King Lear* *Macbeth*
1606		Thomas Middleton's *The Revenger's Tragedy*	*Antony & Cleopatra*
1607			*Coriolanus* *Timon of Athens*
1608		The King's Men lease Blackfriars Theatre.	*Pericles*
1609			*Cymbeline*
1610-11			*The Winter's Tale*

Date	Politics	Other events	Shakespeare
1611-12		Webster's *The White Devil* *King James's Bible*, the Authorised Version in English	*The Tempest*
1613		The Globe burns down. Henslowe opens the Hope Theatre.	*Henry VIII* W.S. buys a house in Blackfriars.
1614		The Globe re-opens. Webster's *The Duchess of Malfi*	
1616			W.S. dies
1623			First Folio of plays is published.

****

Notes:

In this script, the act and scene references in brackets and italics refer to the relevant scene in Shakespeare's *Hamlet*.

The stage directions in the script are Patricia Metham's; Shakespeare's folio texts have very few explicit stage directions or commentary. When reading the text round class, the stage directions should be read out.

Four actors, part of a professional troupe, are on the road and becoming increasingly dispirited about their chances of finding work. They have had to leave the royal castle of Elsinore in a hurry after their performance of a play called *The Mousetrap*, chosen and adapted by Prince Hamlet, was abruptly halted when King Claudius stormed out of the hall, obviously troubled by the action of the play. They decide to act out the events they have themselves witnessed or heard reported, encouraged by the way in which the story follows the pattern of revenge tragedy – a popular convention at the time. As they build their play, they discuss why key characters behaved as they did and what the conflicts, confusions and killings were all about.

DOING HAMLET
Adapted for schools by Patricia Metham

Characters:

1st Player – he is troupe leader

2nd Player - he is an experienced performer, rather impatient and often grumpy

3rd Player – also quite experienced, but easily depressed or made anxious

4th Player – very young and new but immensely keen, patronized by the others

Hamlet - a prince, son of Queen Gertrude and the murdered King Hamlet

Old Hamlet's Ghost – the ghost of Prince Hamlet's father

Horatio – Hamlet's best friend

Polonius – adviser to Claudius, father of Ophelia and Laertes

Laertes – a hot-headed young man, son of Polonius

Ophelia - the innocent and vulnerable daughter of Polonius, in love with Prince Hamlet

King Claudius - brother of the murdered King Hamlet, now married to Queen Gertrude

Gertrude – widow of King Hamlet, mother of Prince Hamlet, newly married to Claudius

Rosencrantz – at university with Prince Hamlet

Guildenstern – like Rosencrantz

Marcello – a courtier and soldier at the Danish court

1st Gravedigger

2nd Gravedigger

Fortinbras – a young warrior-like prince who has a claim to the throne of Denmark

1

Prologue

Enter the four Players, wearing tabards or tunics with a heraldic crest – their liveries. It is important that they are wearing what is, in effect, a uniform since it shows that they are professional actors, under the protection of a noble patron (it is his crest on their tunics) and not simply a band of travelling vagabonds or vagrants, likely to be arrested and punished brutally.

1st Player: Things aren't looking good - we've not had a decent job in weeks. I'm sorry, guys.

2nd Player: Always the same story - 'Don't call us, we'll call you.'

3rd Player: But they never do. If something doesn't turn up soon, I'm packing in this acting lark and getting myself a proper job.

4th Player: We can't just give up.

2nd Player: It's just as well we've still got our liveries and badges to show we're professionals (*points to the crest*) – otherwise we'd be in danger of being picked up as vagrants. And we know what happens to vagrants!

4th Player: Vagrants! Us? No-one could think that – even old Polonius knew we were professionals. What did he call us? 'The tragedians of the city!'

3rd Player: Yeah, maybe – but he's dead now, so he's hardly in a position to vouch for us. And there's no use depending on Hamlet's protection either, no matter how pleased he was to see us – he's dead too.

1st Player: Listen, perhaps we've been going about things the wrong way.

3rd Player: Too right - and I've had enough.

1st Player: No, listen - I mean, perhaps we shouldn't have been trying to be 'walking shadows' in other people's shows, we should be doing our own!

4th Player: You mean, just us - do a play, by ourselves, and hope we can find an audience?

1st Player: Yup. Other people have done it - why not us?

3rd Player: Well, for a start, we haven't got a script.

1st Player: No problem, we'll make it up as we go along. We'll... improvise. All we need is a good story.

2nd Player: All right: how about a nice love story - that always packs them in.

3rd Player: No, no - mystery, that's what we need - death and disaster.

4th Player: And a ghost.

1st Player: A juicy murder, a ghost - and someone out for revenge. Hey, guys, what we're talking about is a Revenge Tragedy. They're very popular. You know where you are with a Revenge Tragedy: you kick off with a murder that has to be avenged, follow that with a great deal of conflict and confusion, and end up with justice being seen to be done and the stage littered with bodies for the final curtain. Always assuming you've got a curtain, that is. It never fails. Right?

2nd Player: Right. (*Long pause.*)

3rd Player: I know...

1st Player: What?

3rd Player: No, no...it wouldn't work.

2nd Player: Try us.

3rd Player: Well, I was thinking... perhaps... "The Mousetrap".

4th Player: I've heard that title somewhere before.

1st Player: Too right - you've been in it before. In fact, it was the last time you were in anything. Remember?

2nd Player: It was a disaster - we never even got paid. I was just getting into my stride when the audience walked out - well, the king did and that rather put the mockers on the whole thing. To say nothing of what happened afterwards.

1st Player: Chaos - that's what happened. I've never seen such goings on - you'd think royalty would know better. Stabbing each other, going mad, ending up with bodies all over the place.

3rd Player: It's a good story. That's what I meant.

2nd Player: Yes, you're right - it's got everything.

3rd Player: And it's ours - we were there! We know what really happened.

4th Player: I'm not so sure - I still find the whole thing very confusing.

3rd Player: All the more reason to do it - we can sort what went on as we go through it - discuss...motivation and ...meaning and ... that sort of thing while we're reliving it all.

1st Player: We'll 'hold a mirror up to nature'. After all, that's what Hamlet himself said 'theatre' is all about.

2nd Player: You're right. Where do we start?

1st Player: We need a prologue, to set the scene. You can do that.

2nd Player: What, me? Right. Give me a bit of space.
'It all happens in Denmark...

3rd Player: Just 'Denmark' won't do - tell them it was at Elsinore, Denmark's answer to the Tower of London - except that it was on a cliff, by the sea.

2nd Player: Do you mind - this is my prologue.
'There was this really excellent king, called Hamlet...

3rd Player: Don't forget he had a brother, Claudius - a very nasty piece of work despite all the charm.

2nd Player: If you interrupt again, I'm likely to do you some damage.

1st Player: Just get on with the story, will you.

2nd Player: Right. Old Hamlet was married to a beautiful queen, called Gertrude.

3rd Player: Gertrude! Not quite in the Cleopatra league of names, if you ask me.

1st Player: No-one did.

2nd Player: They had a son, their pride and joy -

3rd Player: Also called Hamlet. I think that's asking for trouble... All right, all right, pardon me for breathing.

2ⁿᵈ Player: One afternoon Old Hamlet goes for a sleep in the orchard - and wakes up...dead. The Palace announces that he's been bitten by a snake -

3ʳᵈ Player: But WE know the snake looks remarkably like Bad Brother Claudius. Sorry, sorry...you carry on.

2ⁿᵈ Player: So, Prince Hamlet comes back from university for the funeral -

3ʳᵈ Player: Expecting to take over where his dad left off -

2ⁿᵈ Player: But he is very unhappy to discover that his mother has decided to marry his Uncle Claudius before King Hamlet -

4ᵗʰ Player: Young Hamlet's father -

2ⁿᵈ Player: Before the dead King Hamlet is cold in his grave. Prince Hamlet is even more upset to see his wicked Uncle Claudius crowned king -

3ʳᵈ Player: After all, Hamlet is nearly 30, quite old enough to sit on the throne himself.

2ⁿᵈ Player: Imagine his surprise when his best friend, Horatio, tells him that what looks remarkably like the ghost of old King Hamlet has been seen hanging about the castle battlements at night.

3ʳᵈ Player: So young Hamlet decides to go and investigate.

1ˢᵗ Player: (*Has been scribbling furiously during this exchange.*) Right, I've got the basics here. Let's find the rest of the gang and get this show on the road. We'll start on the battlements, with young Hamlet and the Ghost. Come on, we've got things to do.

4ᵗʰ Player: Can I play the Ghost?

2ⁿᵈ Player: You! You'd be a disaster!

4ᵗʰ Player: I really fancy that part.

1ˢᵗ Player: You'll have to grow a bit first. Anyway, we're going to do our own bit in the middle.

4ᵗʰ Player: It's not fair. I never get anything decent to do.

1ˢᵗ Player: Come on – there's work to do, for all of us.   (*They exit.*)

Scene 1 (Act 1, scene 4)

Hamlet first encounters what looks like the ghost of his father.

(Music cue (This is optional but something like the Beatles' 'Yesterday' could set the mood.)
Enter the Ghost, followed by Hamlet and Horatio and Marcello.)

Horatio: It beckons you to go away with it.

   As if it some impartment did desire

   To you alone.

Hamlet: It will not speak, then I will follow it.

Horatio: Do not, my lord.

Hamlet: Why, what should be the fear?

Horatio: What if it should tempt you towards the flood, my lord.

  And draw you to madness? Think of it.

Hamlet: It waves me still. (*To the Ghost*) Go on; I'll follow thee.

Marcello: You shall not go, my lord. (*He catches hold of Hamlet.*)

Hamlet: Hold off your hands. (*He is impatient.*)

Horatio: Be ruled: you shall not go.

Hamlet: Unhand me, gentlemen. (*He pulls out a dagger.*)

  By heaven, I'll make a ghost of him that lets me.

  I say, away! (*To the Ghost*) Go on; I'll follow thee.

(He follows the Ghost off.)

Horatio: He waxes desperate with imagination.

Marcello: Let's follow. 'Tis not fit thus to obey him

Horatio: Have after. To what issue will this come?

Marcello: Something is rotten in the state of Denmark.

Horatio: Heaven will direct it.

Marcello: Nay, let's follow him. *(They exit.)*

(Enter 1ˢᵗ Player and addresses the audience, with 4ᵗʰ Player.)

1ˢᵗ Player: All right so far? Young Hamlet's in a pretty mixed-up state. To give himself a bit of time - and to stop his wicked uncle taking him too seriously - he's going to pretend to be more than a little crazy.

4ᵗʰ Player: Some say he's not pretending - that he really cracks up. Does he?

1ˢᵗ Player: That's for him to know and everyone else to find out. In the meantime, we come to the romantic interest.

(Each character appears as mentioned.)

The old man's called Polonius - he's a sort of Prime Minister. Very full of himself, very keen to be seen as Claudius's right-hand man.

4ᵗʰ Player: You mean he's a bit of a creep.

1ˢᵗ Player: That's his son with him, Laertes - a bit of a lad, our Laertes; can't wait to get away from his father and start living it up in Paris. Polonius is giving him some good advice about how to keep out of trouble.

4ᵗʰ Player: Does he really think Laertes is going to 'be a good boy' once he's in Paris?

1ˢᵗ Player: Yeah, but Polonius sends someone to spy on him and report back.

4ᵗʰ Player: If that's what family life's like at court — well, this court anyway - then I'm glad I'm not part of it!

1ˢᵗ Player: Here's his daughter, Ophelia - a really lovely girl, all heart. In love with young Hamlet — which turns out to be a disaster.

4ᵗʰ Player: What a pity she doesn't have a mother around to watch out for her.

(Players move to one side.)

Scene 2 (Act 1, scene 3)

Polonius gives his son, Laertes, advice and questions Ophelia about Hamlet.

Polonius: Yet here, Laertes! Aboard, aboard, for shame!

    The wind sits in the shoulder of your sail,

    And you are stayed for. There, my blessing with thee.

    And these few precepts in thy memory

    See thou character.

    This above all: to thine own self be true,

    And it must follow as the night the day

    Thou canst not then be false to any man.

    Farewell, my blessing season this in thee.

Laertes: Most humbly do I take my leave, my lord.

    Farewell, Ophelia, and remember well

    What I have said to you. Farewell.   (*Laertes exits.*)

Polonius: What is't, Ophelia, he hath said to you?

Ophelia: So please you, something touching the Lord Hamlet.

Polonius: What is between you? Give me up the truth.

Ophelia: He hath, my lord, of late made many tenders

      Of his affection to me.

Polonius: Affections! Pooh! You speak like a green girl,

      Unsifted in such perilous circumstance.

      Do you believe his 'tenders', as you call them?

Ophelia: My lord, he hath importuned me with love

    In honourable fashion.

Polonius: Ay, 'fashion' you may call it. Go to, go to.

(*They exit.*)

1ˢᵗ Player: Poor innocent, obedient Ophelia. With both her brother and her father telling her not to trust Hamlet, that he's only after one thing - and that, since he's a prince, there's no way he's going to marry her - she agrees to return all his letters.

4ᵗʰ Player: Well, I don't think they'd have stuck together anyway. Strikes me that he needed an older woman, someone who could sort him out. A kind of mother, really.

1ˢᵗ Player: Not like his mother, that's for sure.

4ᵗʰ Player: What happened with the Ghost? Did he ever stop striding about and actually talk to Hamlet?

1ˢᵗ Player: Of course he did, stupid. That's why he'd been allowed out of Purgatory for an hour or two when it was really dark and spooky. Wouldn't be much of a story, would it, if he just stomped about and then disappeared.

(They exit.)

Scene 3 (Act 1, scene 5)

The Ghost tells Hamlet how he was murdered by his brother, who is now king.

(Enter the Ghost followed by Hamlet.)

Hamlet: Whither wilt thou lead me? Speak, I'll go no further.

Ghost: I am thy father's spirit,

Doomed for a certain term to walk the night,

And for the day confin'd to fast in fires.

If thou didst ever thy dear father love -

Hamlet: Oh God!

Ghost: Revenge his foul and most unnatural murder.

Hamlet: Murder!

Ghost: Murder most foul. Now, Hamlet, hear.

'Tis given out that, sleeping in my orchard,

A serpent stung me - but know, thou noble youth,

The serpent that did sting thy father's life

Now wears his crown.

Hamlet: Oh my prophetic soul - my uncle!

Ghost: Taint not thy mind nor let thy soul contrive

Against thy mother aught! Leave her to heaven.

Adieu, adieu, adieu. Remember me.

(Exit Ghost.)

Hamlet: O most pernicious woman!

O villain, villain, smiling damned villain.

(Enter Horatio and Marcello.)

Horatio: What news, my lord?

Hamlet: Give me one poor request.

Horatio: What is't, my lord? We will.

Hamlet: Never make known what you have seen tonight.

Marcello: My lord, we will not.

Hamlet: There are more things in heaven and earth, Horatio,

Than are dreamt of in your philosophy.

The time is out of joint. O cursed spite,

That ever I was born to set it right.

Nay, come, let's go together. *(They exit.)*

(Enter 1st and 4th Players.)

4th Player: Not a happy prince, then.

1st Player: It gets worse. Hamlet grows moodier and moodier. And Claudius gets very suspicious. He's got a guilty conscience, you see, and can't sleep for worrying that Hamlet knows the truth about the old king's death.

4th Player: Why doesn't he just have Hamlet quietly bumped off?

1st Player: Well, of course he'd like to - but Gertrude adores her son and Claudius wants to keep Gertrude happy. Anyway, Hamlet's popular in Denmark, so there's no way he can simply 'disappear' without people wanting to know what's happened to him.

4th Player: You mean Claudius has to pretend he's just worried about Hamlet's health.

1st Player: Polonius thinks he has the answer: Hamlet is mad with love for Ophelia.

4th Player: Okay – so Claudius couldn't quietly murder Hamlet; I get that. Why didn't Hamlet get on with what his father asked him to do – kill Claudius as an act of revenge? There must have been times he could have crept up and stabbed him in the dark.

1st Player: First of all, if he did that straight away this would be one of the shortest Revenge Tragedies in the business. Secondly, he wasn't quite sure that the ghost really was the ghost of his father and not an evil spirit tempting him to commit an unforgivable sin. As far as crimes go, nothing beats killing a king – it's a sure-fire route to Hell.

4th Player: But Claudius . . . .

1st Player: Yup – finally he'll get what he deserves. But not yet.

4th Player: You know what I think Hamlet's problem is – he thinks too much. He's just walking round and round the problem in his head instead of doing something about it.

1st Player: And he even worries about the time he spends worrying! Anyway, he decides he needs to think up some kind of test. That's where we move centre stage.

(Enter 2nd and 3rd Players: 2nd dressed as the Queen and 3rd like Claudius.

They hand 1st a crown and 4th a drum.)

2nd Player: Where have you been? We've been looking for you everywhere.

3rd Player: Yeah – we've got some rehearsing to do, if you don't mind. Doing a gig at the Palace – this could be a big break for us.

1st Player: All right, all right.

(Players' song:

4th Player drums. 1st, 2nd and 3rd Players sing, speak or rap their solo lines as the character they are to play – 1st Player as Old Hamlet, 2nd Player as the Queen and 3rd Player as Claudius. The words matter! The words come from 'The Mousetrap', Act 3, scene 2.)

All: For us and for our tragedy

Here stooping to your clemency

We beg your hearing patiently.

2nd Player: But woe is me, you are so sick of late,

So far from cheer and from your former state.

1st Player: Faith, I must leave thee, love, and shortly, too:

　　　And thou shalt live in this fair world behind.

2nd Player: A second time I kill my husband dead

　　　When second husband kisses me in bed.

1st Player: I do believe you think what now you speak;

　　　　But what we do determine, oft we break.

3rd Player: So think thou wilt no second husband wed,

　　　But die thy thoughts when thy first lord is dead.

All: For us and for our tragedy

　　　Here stooping to your clemency

　　　We beg your hearing patiently.

2nd Player: Here comes Hamlet.

1st Player: He's not happy, but he perks up when he sees us. Bit of an actor himself, young Hamlet.

Scene 4 (Act 2, scene 2)

Hamlet arranges for the Players to act out his father's murder, to see how Claudius reacts.

(Enter Hamlet.)

Hamlet: You are welcome, all. I am glad to see thee well. We'll hear a play tomorrow. Can you play 'The Murder of Gonzago'?

1ˢᵗ Player: Ay, my lord.

Hamlet: We'll have it tomorrow night. You could for a need study a speech of some dozen or sixteen lines, which I would set down and insert in it, could you not?

1ˢᵗ Player: Ay, my lord.

(Players huddle in a group at the side, in whispered conversation.)

Hamlet: (*To himself or direct to the audience*)

I'll have these players

Play out something like the murder of my father

Before mine uncle. I'll observe his looks.

The play's the thing

Wherein I'll catch the conscience of a king.   (*Exit Hamlet.*)

(2ⁿᵈ and 3ʳᵈ Players address the audience.)

3ʳᵈ Player: Claudius has had what he thinks is a neat idea; he's invited two of Hamlet's university friends to Denmark and is asking them to spy on Hamlet, to discover what he knows and whether he is likely to do anything Claudius wouldn't feel happy about.

2ⁿᵈ Player: With friends like Rosencrantz and Guildenstern, Hamlet doesn't need enemies! They are falling over themselves to please Claudius. Take my word for it, they're not very bright, even if they are meant to be students.

(Exit Players.)

Scene 5 (Act 3, scene 1)

Claudius and Polonius listen in to a conversation between Hamlet and Ophelia to see whether Hamlet is mad with love.

(Enter Claudius, Gertrude, Rosencrantz and Guildenstern.)

Claudius: And can you by no drift of conference

    Get from him why he puts on this confusion?

Rosencrantz: He does confess he feels himself distracted

    But from what cause he will by no means speak.

Claudius: Thanks, Rosencrantz and gentle Guildenstern.

Gertrude: Thanks Guildenstern and gentle Rosencrantz.

(Is she correcting Claudius?)

(Rosencrantz and Guildenstern exit.)

Claudius: Sweet Gertrude, leave us, too,

    For we have closely sent for Hamlet hither

    That he, as 'twere by accident, may here

    Affront Ophelia.   *(Exit Gertrude.)*

(Enter Polonius and Ophelia.)

Polonius: Ophelia, walk you here. Read on this book.

    I hear him coming. Let's withdraw, my lord.   *(They hide.)*

(Hamlet enters, talking audibly to himself. He is very agitated, trying to sort out what he is feeling and thinking. He wants a way out of his misery and frustration. He contemplates suicide – 'To be or not to be' - but knows that it is a mortal sin, or was thought to be so in his society. He can't decide whether it might be better, nobler, to endure everything Fate throws at him. He imagines himself putting on full armour and wading into the sea to fight the waves – knowing that he would make no impression on the water but would be drowned, which would put an end to his troubles.)

(Hamlet thinks death may be just like falling quietly and calmly asleep - but then he is afraid of the dreams he might have.)

Hamlet: To be or not to be, that is the question:

Whether it be nobler in the mind to suffer

The slings and arrows of outrageous fortune,

Or to take arms against a sea of troubles

And by opposing end them. To die - to sleep,

No more; and by a sleep to say we end

The heart-ache and the thousand natural shocks

That flesh is heir to: 'tis a consummation

Devoutly to be wish'd. To die - to sleep;

To sleep, perchance to dream - ay, there's the rub,

For in that sleep of death what dreams may come...

(We do not hear the rest; he hums to himself as he walks across the stage, deep in thought. Claudius and Polonius strain to overhear him.)

(Ophelia looks increasingly nervous, until she can bear it no longer. She's clearly very frightened, which makes Hamlet suspicious.)

Ophelia: Good my lord,

How does your honour for this many a day?

Hamlet: Ha! (*Alerted by her evident terror and the way she is glancing towards the curtain behind which her father and Claudius are hiding, he realizes that they are being spied on. He thinks she may be part of a conspiracy against him.*)

Are you honest?

Ophelia: My lord?

Hamlet: Go to, I'll no more on't, it hath made me mad.

(He directs these comments to where he has guessed Polonius and Claudius are hiding. He makes a clear death threat to Claudius as being the one already married who will not be allowed to live. He sounds not only violent but mentally unbalanced.)

I say we will have no more marriage. Those that are married already - all but one – shall live; the rest shall keep as they are.

(*To Ophelia – urging her to escape from this corrupt and dangerous court, to the one place a vulnerable girl might be safe.*) To a nunnery, go!

(*Exit Hamlet.*)

Ophelia: O, what a noble mind is here o'erthrown! O woe is me

To have seen what I have seen, see what I see… (*She is crying.*)

(*Claudius and Polonius come out of hiding.*)

Claudius: Love? His affections do not that way tend,

Nor what he spake, though it lack'd form a little,

Was not like madness. He shall with speed to England.

What think you on't?

Polonius: It shall do well. But yet I do believe

The origin and commencement of his grief

Sprung from neglected love. How now, Ophelia?

You need not tell us what Lord Hamlet said,

We heard it all. (*Ophelia runs out, crying.*) My lord, do you as you please,

But if you hold it fit, after the play

Let his queen-mother all alone entreat him

To show his grief, let her be round with him,

And I'll be plac'd, so please you, in the ear

Of all their conference. If she find him not,

To England send him; or confine him where

Your wisdom shall best think.

Claudius: It shall be so.

Madness in great ones must not unwatch'd go.

(*Exit Claudius and Polonius.*)

(Music cue - optional)

(Enter 2nd Player, still dressed as a Queen, looking flustered. He addresses the audience.)

2nd Player: This is our big moment - we're all set to give the performance of a lifetime. It's a good story - murder and betrayal. Not quite as it was originally written - Hamlet's put in something extra. He's paying, so we do as we're told and don't ask questions.

I'm the queen - and I'm very nervous. Me - who never gets stage fright! There's something about this whole set up that makes my skin crawl. It's like that really heavy feeling you get just before a killer thunder storm. Oh, here comes Hamlet - last minute director's notes, I expect.

Scene 5 (Act 3, scene 2)

The Players act out King Hamlet's murder and Hamlet is convinced that his uncle Claudius is guilty – the play is called 'The Mousetrap'.

(Enter Hamlet with the other three Players.)

Hamlet: Speak the speech, I pray you, as I pronounced it to you, trippingly
on the tongue; but if you mouth it as many of your players do, I had as lief
the town-crier spoke my lines. I pray you avoid it.

1ˢᵗ Player: I warrant your Honour.

Hamlet: Be not too tame neither, but let your own discretion be your
tutor. Suit the action to the word, the word to the action, with this special
observance, that you o'erstep not the modesty of nature. For anything so
o'erdone is from the purpose of playing, whose end, both at the first and
now, was and is to hold as 'twere the mirror up to nature. Go make you
ready.   *(All the Players exit.)*

(Hamlet calls out for Horatio, who comes in.)

Horatio: Here, sweet lord, at your service.

Hamlet: There is a play tonight before the King;
One scene of it comes near the circumstance
Which I have told thee of my father's death.
I prithee, when thou seest that act afoot,
Observe my uncle. Give him heedful note;
For I mine eyes will rivet to his face,
And after we will both our judgments join
In censure of his seeming.

Horatio: Well, my lord.

Hamlet: They are coming to the play. I must be idle.
Get you a place.

(Enter Claudius, Gertrude, Ophelia, Horatio, Rosencrantz and Guildenstern. They prepare to watch the play. Hamlet's agitation is clear to see. He pulls Ophelia towards him; she looks terrified. He may force her to sit down, and sit on the floor beside her, or hold her close to him in a way that obviously makes her uncomfortable. As the play begins, Hamlet's intense gaze shifts backwards and forwards from Claudius to the players.)

(When deciding how to stage this, keep in mind that the audience must be able to see how Claudius reacts and how Hamlet is behaving, as well as being able to see the Players as they perform. Horatio must also be able to see Claudius as well as the Players.)

(The following mime is accompanied by music: 'Nobody Knows the Trouble I've Seen', a Negro Spiritual, works well - or the Beatles' 'A Long and Winding Road'.)

(4th Player sits by the side, drumming. Enter 1st Player, dressed as a king, arm in arm with the 2nd Player as Queen. They show each other great affection. The Player King lies down to rest; the Player Queen blows him a kiss then runs off. All the players' actions need to be very exaggerated, very theatrical. Claudius has begun to look uneasy, fidgety.)

Hamlet: How like you this play?

Claudius: What do you call the play?

Hamlet: 'The Mousetrap'. Tis a knavish piece of work, but what of that? Your Majesty, and we that have free souls, it touches us not.

(Enter 3rd Player as the Poisoner. He looks about him furtively, gets out a small bottle, carefully pours poison into the Player King's ear and exits. The Player King writhes in agony and dies.)

(The Player Queen returns and appears distraught, weeping over her husband's body. The Poisoner returns with a flashy ring, which he offers her. She smiles, picks up the dead King's crown, gives it to the Poisoner and they go off, arm in arm.)

(Gertrude looks alarmed. Claudius gets up, clearly agitated.)

Ophelia: The King rises.

Hamlet: What, frighted with false fire?

Gertrude: How fares my lord?

Polonius: Give o'er the play.

(The Player King gets up and exits, followed by 4ᵗʰ Player.)

Claudius: Give me some light. Away.

(All leave, except Hamlet and Horatio.)

Hamlet: O, Horatio, I'll take the Ghost's word for a thousand pounds. Didst perceive?

Horatio: Very well, my lord.

(Enter Rosencrantz and Guildenstern.)

Guildenstern: The Queen your mother, in most great affliction of spirit, hath sent me to you.

Hamlet: My mother, you say -

Rosencrantz: Then thus she says – your behaviour hath struck her into amazement and admiration.

Hamlet: O wonderful son that can so astonish a mother. But is there no sequel at the heels of this mother's admiration? Impart.

Rosencrantz: She desires to speak with you in her closet ere you go to bed.

Hamlet: We shall obey, were she ten times our mother. Have you any further trade with us?

Rosencrantz: Good my lord, what is the cause of your distemper?

Hamlet: Sir, I lack advancement.

Rosencrantz: How can that be, when you have the voice of the king himself for your succession in Denmark?

Hamlet: (*Producing a recorder.*) Will you play upon this pipe?

Guildenstern: My lord, I cannot.

Hamlet: I pray you.

Guildenstern: Believe me, I cannot.

Hamlet: I do beseech you.

Guildenstern: I know no touch of it, my lord.

Hamlet: 'Tis as easy as lying.

Guildenstern: I have not the skill. (*He sounds very defensive and nervous.*)

Hamlet: Why look you now, how unworthy a thing you make of me. You would play upon me, you would seem to know my stops. Do you think I am easier to be played upon than a pipe? (*They all exit.*)

(*Enter Players.*)

1st Player: So Hamlet goes off to talk to his mother in her bedroom, not knowing that old Polonius is hiding behind a curtain to listen. Hamlet wants to make Gertrude feel bad about getting married again only a few weeks after his father's mysterious death, and to feel particularly bad about marrying her dead husband's brother.

3rd Player: This, you understand, was not generally considered a 'proper' thing to do; some people called it 'incest' - and quoted from the Bible to prove it. They said no good would ever come of it. Well, you think of Henry VIII; he started off by 'doing a Claudius', you might say - he married his dead brother's wife - and it was all downhill after that as far as wives went, and no mistake.

2nd Player: Anyway, back to Denmark. Claudius - now really worried - is plotting with Rosencrantz and Guildenstern to send Hamlet to England and to have him killed by the English king, who happens to owe Claudius a favour.

1st Player: Gertrude is very upset.

3rd Player: Hamlet, on the other hand, is on a high - drunk with excitement - which makes him more than a little frightening. (*Exit Players.*)

Scene 6 (Act 3, scene 4)

Hamlet accuses his mother of betraying his father and then stabs Polonius, who has been eavesdropping, believing it to be Claudius.

(Polonius enters and hides. Use music to heighten the emotion of this scene. The 'stabbing' music from Hitchcock's film 'Psycho' could work well when Hamlet stabs Polonius through the curtain. Enter Hamlet and Gertrude. Hamlet is carrying a dagger and clearly very angry.)

Gertrude: Hamlet, thou hast thy father much offended.

Hamlet: Mother, you have my father much offended.

    You are the Queen, your husband's brother's wife,

    And, I would it were not so, you are my mother.

Gertrude: Nay, then I'll set those to you that can speak.

Hamlet: *(He forces her to sit down.)*

    Come, come, and sit you down, you shall not budge.

    You go not till I set you up a glass

    Where you may see the inmost part of you.

(He grabs a small mirror and thrusts it at her face, while holding the dagger in a threatening way.)

Gertrude: What wilt thou do? Thou wilt not murder me? Help!

Polonius: *(Behind curtain)* What ho! Help!

Hamlet: How now! A rat! Dead!   *(He stabs Polonius through the curtain.)*

Polonius: I am slain!

Gertrude: O me, what hast thou done?

Hamlet: Nay, I know not. Is it the King?   *(Polonius falls into view.)*

Gertrude: O what a rash and bloody deed is this!

Hamlet: A bloody deed. Almost as bad, good mother,

    As kill a king and marry with his brother.

Gertrude: As kill a king?

Hamlet: Ay, lady, it was my word.

(Enter Ghost.)

Ghost: Do not forget! This visitation

Is but to whet thy almost blunted purpose.

Gertrude: Whereon do you look?

Hamlet: On him, on him. Look you how pale he glares.

Do you see nothing there?

Gertrude: Nothing at all - yet all that is I see.

Hamlet: Why, look you there, look how it steals away.

My father, in his habit as he liv'd.   *(Exit Ghost.)*

Gertrude: O Hamlet, thou hast cleft my heart in twain.

Hamlet: *(He takes hold of Polonius's body by the legs.)*

Good night. But go not to my uncle's bed.

For this same lord

I do repent; but heaven hath pleased it so,

To punish me with this, and this with me.

I must to England, you know that?

Gertrude: Alack, I had forgot. 'Tis so concluded on.

Hamlet: There's letters sealed, and my two schoolfellows,

Whom I will trust as I will adders fanged -

They bear the mandate, they must sweep my way

And marshal me to knavery. Let it work.

This man shall set me packing.

I'll lug the guts into the neighbouring room.

Good night, mother.

(Hamlet drags Polonius off one way and Gertrude goes off slowly the other way, crying.)

Scene 7 (Act 4, scene 2)

Hamlet again evades questions from Rosencrantz and Guildenstern.

(Hamlet returns.)

Hamlet: Safely stowed.

Rosencrantz and Guildenstern: *(Off-stage)* Hamlet! Lord Hamlet!

Hamlet: What noise? Who calls on Hamlet? O, here they come.

(Enter Rosencrantz and Guildenstern.)

Rosencrantz: What have you done, my lord, with the dead body?

Guildenstern: Tell us where it is, that we may take it thence, and bear it to the chapel.

Hamlet: Do not believe it.

Rosencrantz: Believe what?

Hamlet: That I can keep your counsel and not mine own. Besides, to be demanded of by a sponge! What replication should be made by the son of a king?

Rosencrantz: Take you me for a sponge, my lord?

Hamlet: Ay sir, that soaks up the king's countenance, his rewards, his authorities. When he needs what you have gleaned, it is but squeezing you and, sponge, you shall be dry again.

Rosencrantz: I understand you not, my lord.

Hamlet: I'm glad of it. A knavish speech sleeps in a foolish ear.

Rosencrantz: My lord, you must tell us where the body is, and go with us to the king.

Hamlet: The body is with the king, but the king is not with the body. The king is a thing.

Guildenstern: A thing, my lord?

Hamlet: Of nothing. Bring me to him.   *(They exit.)*

(Enter all four Players.)

1st Player: Right, let's move it along a bit. So, where are we?

2nd Player: Left looking like lemons, if you ask me! I've never had an audience walk out on me before.

4th Player: What's supposed to happen to us? Suddenly we're nobodies.

2nd Player: So much for Hamlet's being pleased to see us! Will he 'be pleased to see' we're paid? I don't think so!

3rd Player: Hamlet's got enough problems of his own. If Claudius has his way, it'll be a one-way ticket to England for Hamlet.

4th Player: I suppose we just keep our heads down and hope everybody forgets about us.

2nd Player: It's Ophelia I feel sorry for; big brother having a good time in Paris while she's left in Denmark with a lover-boy who's behaving very oddly - going so far, in fact, as to stab her old dad. No wonder she cracks up.

3rd Player: Just look at her - breaks your heart, doesn't it! You can see why Laertes goes ballistic when he gets home and discovers what's been going on.

1st Player: He's desperate for revenge on whoever has done such damage to his family.

(The Players stand aside.)

Scene 8 (Act 4, scene 5)

In which Ophelia is seen, distracted and grieving, and Laertes returns, determined to get revenge for what has been done to his family.

(Enter Ophelia, Gertrude and Claudius. Ophelia has had a mental breakdown. She is in a nightmare world of her own; her words and her singing are all linked to her father's murder.)

Gertrude: How now Ophelia?

Ophelia: (*Sings*) How should I your true love know

From another one?

By his cockle hat and staff

And his sandal shoon.

Gertrude: Alas, sweet lady, what imports this song?

Ophelia: (*Sings*) He is dead and gone, lady,

He is dead and gone,

At his head a grass-green turf,

At his heels a stone.

Claudius: How long hath she been thus?

Ophelia: I hope all will be well. We must be patient. But I cannot choose but weep to think they would lay him in the cold ground. My brother shall know of it.   *(Exit Ophelia.)*

Claudius: O, this is the poison of deep grief: it springs

All from her father's death.

Her brother is in secret come from France.

(Laertes bursts in.)

Laertes: O thou vile king,

Give me my father.

Gertrude: Calmly, good Laertes.

Claudius: Let him go, Gertrude. Tell me, Laertes,

Why thou art this incens'd. Let him go, Gertrude.

Speak, man.   (*An eight-beat pause – what is happening?*)

Laertes: Where is my father?

Claudius: Dead.

Gertrude: But not by him (*indicating Claudius*).

Laertes: His means of death, his obscure funeral –

Cry to be heard, as 'twere from heaven to earth,

That I must call't in question.

Claudius: So you shall.

And where th'offence is, let the great axe fall.

I pray you go with me.

(Gertrude, Claudius and Laertes exit.)

1st Player: Laertes is in no state to think clearly.

4th Player: You can't blame him.

3rd Player: And Claudius is a pretty smooth talker - by the time he's finished, he's got Laertes agreeing to kill Hamlet, if the King of England doesn't do it first.

1st Player: Which, of course, he doesn't. Hamlet never gets as far as England.

2nd Player: You remember how Hamlet feels about Rosencrantz and Guildenstern - he trusts them as he would "adders fanged" - well, while they're asleep, he opens the letter Claudius gave them and does a nifty bit of forgery, so that the message to the King of England now reads: "Kill these two men." No mention of Hamlet himself!

3rd Player: They get what they deserve, I suppose.

1st Player: Then, believe it or not, Hamlet is captured by pirates.

2nd Player: Pirates - I ask you!

1st Player: A lucky coincidence, I'll admit, but that's what happens. They even bring him back to Denmark, just in time for Ophelia's funeral.

4ᵗʰ Player: Poor Ophelia - falls into a river and drowns.

2ⁿᵈ Player: Probably the best thing for her - she didn't have much of a future, if you think about it.

3ʳᵈ Player: One more thing for Laertes to blame Hamlet for.

1ˢᵗ Player: He'll stop at nothing to see Hamlet dead - he'll even play dirty himself, at Claudius's suggestion, of course.

3ʳᵈ Player: But that comes later. After the funeral – and what a shambles that was!

Scene 9 (Act 5, scene 1)

Hamlet turns up at Ophelia's funeral.

(Enter two gravediggers. They are discussing whether or not Ophelia should have a Christian burial since she might have committed suicide by drowning herself. Although they are comic characters, the question would have been a serious one for Shakespeare's audience, who would have considered suicide a mortal sin. The gravediggers decide that there is one law for the upper class and another for common people.)

1st Gravedigger: Is she to be buried in Christian burial, when she willfully seeks her own salvation?

2nd Gravedigger: I tell thee she is, therefore make her grave straight. The crowner hath sat on her and finds it Christian burial.

1st Gravedigger: How can that be, unless she drowned herself in her own defense?

2nd Gravedigger: Will you ha' the truth an't? If this had not been a gentlewoman, she should have been buried out o' Christian burial.

1st Gravedigger: Come, my spade. Go, fetch me a stoup of liquor.

(Exit 2nd Gravedigger. Enter Hamlet and Horatio.)

1st Gravedigger: (*Sings*) In youth when I did love, did love,

Methought it was very sweet. (*He throws up a skull.*)

Hamlet: Whose grave is this, sirrah?

1st Gravedigger: Mine, sir.

Hamlet: What man dost thou dig it for?

1st Gravedigger: For no man, sir.

Hamlet: Who is to be buried in it?

1st Gravedigger: One that was a woman, sir: but, rest her soul, she's dead.

Hamlet: How long hast thou been a gravemaker?

1st Gravedigger: It was that very day that young Hamlet was born - he that is mad and sent into England.

Hamlet: Why was he sent into England?

1st Gravedigger: Why, because he was mad. He shall recover his wits there. Or if he do not, 'tis no great matter there.

Hamlet: Why?

1st Gravedigger: 'Twill not be seen in him there. There the men are as mad as he.

Hamlet: (*He picks up the skull.*) Whose was this?

1st Gravedigger: This same skull, sir, was Yorrick's skull, the King's jester.

Hamlet: Alas, poor Yorrick. I knew him, Horatio, a fellow of infinite jest, of most excellent fancy. (*To the skull.*) Where be your gibes now, your gambols, your songs, your flashes of merriment, that were wont to set the table on a roar? Not one now to mock your own grinning? But soft. Here comes the King.   (*Hamlet and Horatio hide.*)

(*A funeral procession enters, with Ophelia's body, which is laid in the grave (on the ground?). Claudius, Gertrude and Laertes are there.*)

Hamlet: What, the fair Ophelia!

Gertrude: (*Scattering flowers on the body.*)

Sweets to the sweet. Farewell.

I hoped thou should'st have been my Hamlet's wife:

I thought thy bride-bed to have deck'd, sweet maid,

And not have strew'd thy grave.

Laertes: Hold off the earth awhile,

Till I have caught her once more in mine arms.

Hamlet: (*He leaps forward and tries to pull Laertes away from Ophelia.*)

I lov'd Ophelia. Forty thousand brothers

Could not with their quantity of love

Make up my sum. What wilt thou do for her?

Claudius: O, he is mad, Laertes.

Gertrude: This is mere madness.

Claudius: I pray thee, good Horatio, wait upon him.

(Horatio drags Hamlet off. All except the Players exit.)

1st Player: We're almost finished. Just the final sorting out to do.

4th Player: They all end up dead, don't they?

3rd Player: No, no - that's not what I remember. I think Horatio gets away. Doesn't he?

1st Player: He doesn't want to, but Hamlet begs him to stay alive and make sure that everyone gets to know the truth about … well, about all this.

2nd Player: So why are we bothering, then?

3rd Player: You've seen Horatio - nice enough, but hardly up to our standard when it comes to performance! Hamlet just didn't remember about us as he was gasping his last. If he'd had time to think, I'm sure he'd have asked us.

2nd Player: If you say so.

3rd Player: Let's get on with it then. The Grand Finale.

(Music cue)

1st Player: Claudius and Laertes have set a trap for Hamlet. Laertes challenges him to a fencing contest, but poisons his own rapier and takes the button off the tip so that he can really do some damage.

3rd Player: Claudius puts poison into a cup of wine that he plans to give Hamlet if Laertes doesn't kill him first.

4th Player: Does Gertrude know about all this?

3rd Player: Shouldn't think so - she adores Hamlet, even if he does give her headaches. I think she only really understands what's being going on when she gets hold of the poisoned wine and sees Claudius panic. Then she deliberately sacrifices herself to save her son.

2ⁿᵈ Player: On the other hand, she could really fancy a drink and be annoyed by Claudius trying to stop her.

1ˢᵗ Player: You might as well ask if she knowingly married her husband's murderer.

4ᵗʰ Player: Well, yes, exactly. Did she?

3ʳᵈ Player: Sort it out for yourself. We've got to get on.

Scene 10 (Act 5, scene 2)

The final scene – in which Claudius's treachery is revealed, Gertrude drinks poison meant for Hamlet, and Hamlet and Laertes kill each other and forgive each other.

(Music cue - something like Walton's 'Crown Imperial' would work well).

(Enter Claudius, Gertrude, Laertes, Hamlet and Horatio, with great ceremony. Marcello acts as referee for the fight.)

Marcello: Round One!

(Hamlet and Laertes duel.)

Marcello: A hit, a very palpable hit.

Laertes: Well, again. *(They fight.)*

Claudius: Stay, give me drink. *(2nd Player passes him a cup.)*

Claudius: Hamlet, this pearl is thine. (*He drops something into the wine.*) Give him the cup.

Hamlet: I'll play this bout first. Set it by awhile. (*Hamlet and Laertes duel.*) Another hit. What say you?

Laertes: I do confess it.

Gertrude: (*Taking the poisoned cup.*) The Queen carouses to thy fortune, Hamlet.

Claudius: Gertrude, do not drink.

(Pause - during the five beats of silence that Shakespeare has written into the 10-beat iambic line, it must be made clear whether or not Gertrude suddenly recognizes that Claudius is as evil as Hamlet has claimed and that there is something very wrong with the wine she is holding. If she understands that, then her decision to drink the wine is heroic; she sacrifices herself to save her son. In that case, as what she knows will be her final words to him, it may be Hamlet she asks to pardon her – for not believing him when he spoke of his father being murdered and for continuing to stay beside Claudius despite Hamlet's opposition. However, she could simply be determined to have the wine because she likes wine

and is annoyed by her husband telling her what not to do, so her reply is to him in a challenging kind of way.)

Gertrude: I will, my lord, I pray you pardon me.

Claudius: (*To himself*) It is the poison'd cup. It is too late.

Laertes: Have at you now!

(Laertes catches Hamlet off guard and wounds him. Enraged, Hamlet fights furiously, knocking the sword from Laertes's hand - he throws Laertes his own sword, picks up the poisoned one and continues fighting.)

(Claudius has been watching Gertrude with horror, knowing what is about to happen. The Queen collapses.)

3rd Player: Look to the Queen!

(In the confusion, Hamlet wounds Laertes.)

Horatio: They bleed on both sides. How is, my lord?

Marcello: How is it, Laertes?

Laertes: I am killed with mine own treachery.

Hamlet: How does the Queen?

Claudius: She swoons to see them bleed.

Gertrude: No, no, the drink, the drink! O my dear Hamlet,

The drink, the drink! I am poisoned.

Hamlet: O villainy! Let the door be locked. Treachery! Seek it out!

Laertes: It is here, Hamlet. Hamlet, thou art slain.

No medicine in the world can do thee good;

In thee there's not half an hour's life.

The treacherous instrument is in thy hand,

Unbated and envenomed. The foul practice

Hath turned itself on me. Lo, here I lie,

Never to rise again. Thy mother's poison'd.

I can no more. The King - the King's to blame!

Hamlet: The point envenomed too! Then, venom, to thy work.

(He wounds Claudius.)

Players: Treason! Treason!

Claudius: O yet defend me, friends. I am but hurt.

Hamlet: Here, thou incestuous, murderous, damned Dane,

Drink off this potion. Follow my mother.

(Hamlet forces the wine down Claudius's throat. Claudius dies.)

Laertes: He is justly served.

It is a poison tempered by himself.

Exchange forgiveness with me, noble Hamlet.

Mine and my father's death come not upon thee,

Nor thine on me.   *(He dies.)*

Hamlet: Heaven make thee free of it. I follow thee.

I am dead, Horatio. Wretched Queen, adieu.

Horatio, I am dead, thou livest.

Report me and my cause aright to the unsatisfied. *(Music cue.)*

What warlike noise is that?

1ˢᵗ Player: Young Fortinbras, with conquest come from Poland.

4ᵗʰ Player: Who?

3ʳᵈ Player: Don't worry about it - he's a neighbouring prince with lots of energy and soldiers, looking for a country to be king of.

2ⁿᵈ Player: It's like this: years back, young Hamlet's father, old King Hamlet, killed his father, old King Fortinbras, and took over his kingdom - so young Fortinbras has a score to settle.

4ᵗʰ Player: I don't think I want to know.

3ʳᵈ Player: This could be his lucky day.

Hamlet: O, I die, Horatio.

> The potent poison quite o'ercrows my spirit,
>
> But I do prophesy th'election lights
>
> On Fortinbras. He has my dying voice.
>
> So tell him - the rest is silence.   (*Hamlet dies.*)

Horatio: Now cracks a noble heart. Good night, sweet prince,

> And flights of angels sing thee to thy rest.

(*Enter Fortinbras, with soldiers.*)

Fortinbras: Where is this sight?

Horatio: What is it you would see?

> If aught of woe or wonder, cease your search.

Fortinbras: Bear Hamlet like a soldier to the stage,

> For he was likely, had he been put on,
>
> To have proved most royal; and for his passage,
>
> The soldier's music and the rite of war speak loudly for him.

(*Fortinbras and Horatio exit, with soldiers carrying out Hamlet's body to solemn military music.*)

4th Player: Is that it?

2nd Player: What a story! You name it, it's got it: love, betrayal, death, ghosts, a play within a play, which is very clever, and even a bit of down to earth - not to say 'in the earth' - comedy.

3rd Player: And it's got sword-play. Audiences love that!

2nd Player: I think we could be onto a winner.

1st Player: Well, what are we waiting for - let's go and make our fortunes, back in the city.

> Someone else can clear up here.

(They leave, singing)

All: For us and for our tragedy
　　Here stooping to your clemency
　　We beg your hearing patiently.

****

Other titles available in this series:

Trying Macbeth

ISBN: 978-1-9161361-2-0

Available shortly:

Just As You Like It

On Twelfth Night

Loving Romeo & Juliet